Blue Animals On The Planet

Blue has long been
considered the world's most
popular favorite color, even
though it's the rarest occuring
pigment found in nature.
Its tendency to appear in
animals is fairly uncommon.

BLUE LINCKIA

is a species of sea star in the shallow waters of tropical Indo-Pacific. These sea stars may grow up to 30 cm in diameter. The variation most commonly found is pure, dark, or light blue, although observers find the aqua, purple, or orange variation throughout the ocean.

HYACINTH MACAW

is a parrot native to central and eastern South America. It is the largest macaw and the largest flying parrot species. The majority of the hyacinth macaw diet is nuts,from native palms, such as acuri and bocaiuva palms.

BLUE LOBSTER

is a species of freshwater crayfish endemic to Florida. The protein and a red carotenoid molecule known as astaxanthin combine to form a blue complex known as crustacyanin, giving the lobster its blue color. An estimated one in 2 million lobsters are blue.

REGAL TANG

is a member of the surgeonfish family. The Regal Tang has a royal blue body, yellow tail, and black 'palette' design. Regals occur naturally in the western Pacific. They are common throughout the Great Barrier Reef of Australia.

BLUE POISON DART FROG

is a medium-sized frog that weighs about 8 grams and grows to 3.0-4.5 cm in length. The Blue Poison Dart Frog feeds on ants, beetles, flies, mites, spiders, termites, maggots and caterpillars.

MENELAUS BLUE MORPHO

is a very large butterfly, with a wingspan of approximately 138 mm. The adult males have brighter colours than the females. Morpho butterflies are Neotropical butterflies found mostly in Central America as well as Mexico and South America.

CARPATHIAN BLUE SLUG

This slug turns blue when an adult and becomes 100 – 140 mm in length. Carpathian blue slug inhabits deciduous and coniferous forests in mountains, usually at the bottom, or under dead wood logs.

RIBBON EEL

is a species of moray eel. The ribbon eel is found in lagoons and reefs in the Indo-Pacific ocean. The blue adult males range from 65 to 94 cm in length, while the larger yellow females can reach up to 130 cm.

WESTERN BLUEBIRD

is a small thrush, about 15 to 18 cm in length. Male Western Bluebirds are shiny blue above with rust-orange extending from a vest on the breast onto the upper back. Females are gray-buff with a pale orange wash on the breast and blue tints to the wings and tail.

BLUE DASHER

is one of the most
commonly sighted
dragonflies in all
of North America.
The blue dasher
grows up to 25-43
mm long. They are
found by ponds,
lakes, marshes, and
bogs. They can also
be found in almost
aywhere when there
is still water.

BLUE PEAFOWL

is a large and brightly coloured bird, is a species of peafowl native to South Asia. Blue peafowl lives mainly on the ground in open forest or on land under cultivation where they forage for berries, grains but also prey on snakes, lizards, and small rodents.

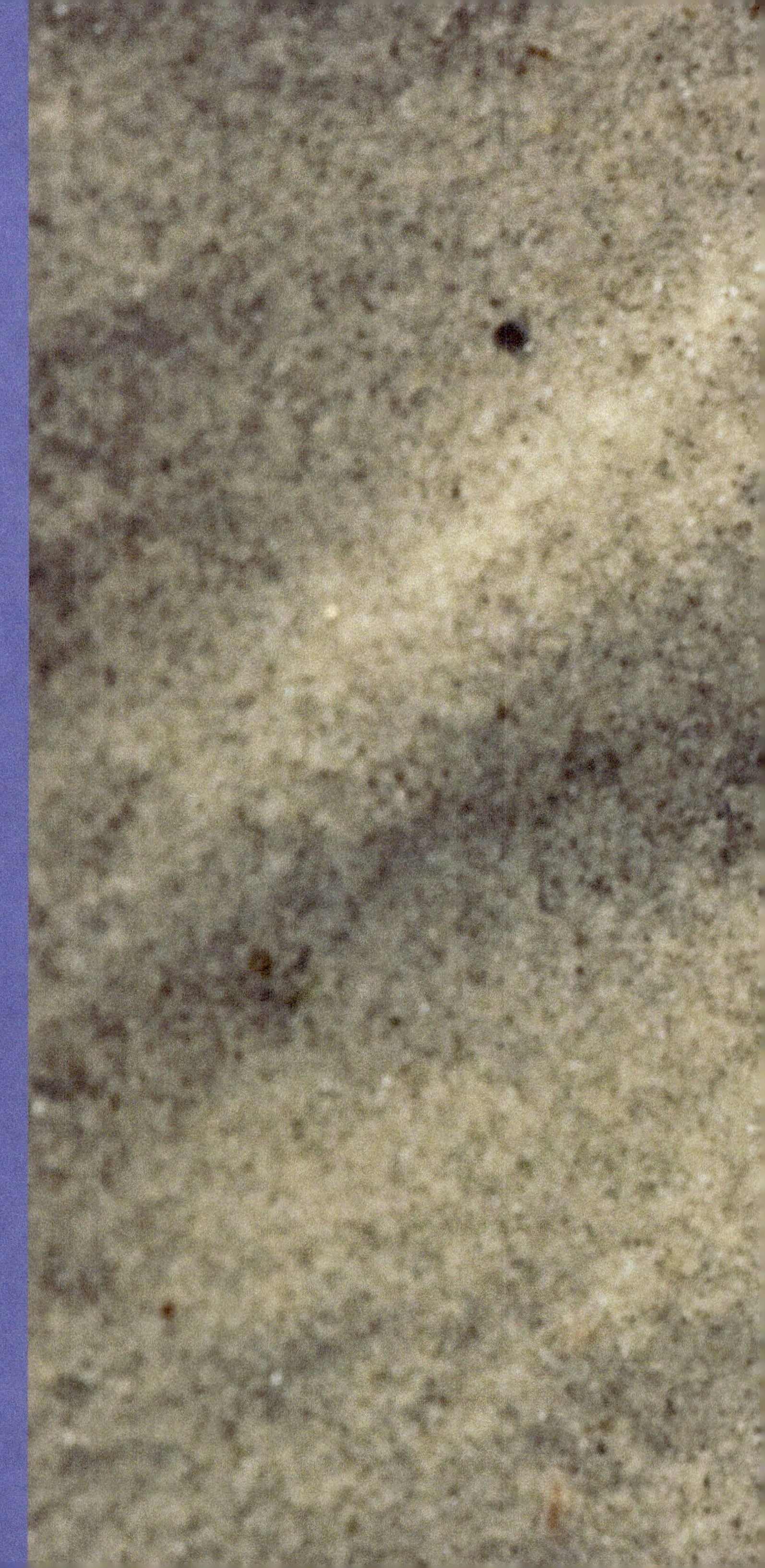

BLUE MUSSEL

is a hinged, filter-feeding bivalve found in Rhode Island waters. The shape of the shell is triangular and elongate with rounded edges. The blue mussel is able to withstand great temperature extremes, including freezing, excessive heat, and drought.

DWARF GOURAMI

is a species of gourami native to Pakistan, India and Bangladesh. This species can reach a length of 8.8 cm. Most dwarf gouramis live for about four years.

BLUE AGAMA

is active during daytime and feeds on insects and other arthropods and plants. During the breeding season, males become a striking blue colour to attract females.